EVERYDAY ADVENTURES

>TINY QUESTS TO SPARK YOUR CREATIVE LIFE<

A JOURNAL
BY TAMMY STROBEL

"I feel like **Everyday Adventures** *was made for me. As I continue to embrace slow living, I find myself observing my surroundings and becoming more mindful of what I bring into every space and situation. This journal is the perfect companion for that, as it helps me document my adventures and learn more about myself through the process. I'm so grateful Tammy made this and put it out into the world."*

—Cait Flanders | caitflanders.com

"Tammy reminds us that we don't need to travel thousands of miles for true adventure. Sometimes, the grandest experiences can be found right under our feet. This whimsical and inspiring journal will wake you up to the wanderlust that is here and now."

—Amanda Sandlin | www.amandasandlin.com

"This journal/adventure guide will encourage you see the world and your heart. All you have to do is open the book and step outside your front door. Tammy's beautiful words and images will inspire you to create your own views and help you capture the special moments you experience on your everyday adventures."

—Courtney Carver | bemorewithless.com

"In Everyday Adventures, *Tammy Strobel reminds us that we don't have to stray far from our homes to get off the beaten path—or appreciate our lives. Adventure abounds when we open our minds, and our hearts, to exploring local possibilities. And sometimes we don't even have to leave the house! Using twelve thoughtful exercises, Tammy encourages us to be mindful of our thoughts and intentional with our time while we record our own Everyday Adventures in our journal and with our cameras."*

—Holly Clark | hollyclarkphotography.com

This Journal Belongs To:

_____

IN THIS JOURNAL

INTRODUCTION

"Your life is your art."
—Keri Smith

Shortly before my fifth birthday, in 1982, my mom and I flew to Taipei, Taiwan to visit friends. I only have a few distinct memories of our travels in Taiwan. I remember the giant plane we flew on and the My Little Pony coloring books my mom brought for me to play with on the flight. One memory involves getting my hair and nails done at a local salon and I also remember walking through the city streets with our friends. When I looked up at the big buildings, my stomach tossed and turned. I remember feeling very small in a big city.

In addition to visiting Taiwan, I traveled with my mom to Alaska as well as New York, Maine, Vermont, and New Hampshire. My mom grew up in Loudonville, New York, so we traveled to the east coast to visit family frequently. These types of adventures instilled a love of traveling in me. As an adult, my fondness for travel has not dissipated. It's only grown stronger as I've aged.

However, I've found that I don't have to visit faraway places to experience the joy of traveling. For instance, I've discovered dozens of magical places near my home in Siskiyou County,

California. My husband, Logan, and I take frequent day and weekend trips because we love exploring northern California. Exploring local sights reminds me that my adventures can be tiny, yet extraordinary!

With gratitude,
Tammy Strobel

RowdyKittens.com
Instagram: @RowdyKittens

HOW TO USE THIS JOURNAL

Everyday Adventures is part guidebook and part journal. It includes twelve tiny quests that are designed to spark your creative life. In addition, the book will help you:

> » Explore what your community has to offer
> » Document your adventures
> » Enjoy tiny beautiful moments
> » Find beauty and magic anywhere

Finally, this guidebook/journal is meant to be well loved. Don't let this book sit on your shelf. Instead, carry it everywhere—especially on your everyday adventures.

Use the notebook to record observations about your daily adventures with words, photos, drawings, watercolors, or whatever medium moves you. Remember there are no journaling rules, just suggestions.

With that, let's dive into your first tiny quest—*Prepare for your adventure by gathering your tools.*

1 | PREPARE FOR YOUR ADVENTURE BY GATHERING YOUR TOOLS.

"Adventures don't begin until you get into the forest. That first step is an act of faith."
—Mickey Hart, Grateful Dead drummer

No matter where you're going, whether it's a coffee shop or on a long day hike, don't forget to gather your tools before you leave the house. Always ask yourself: *What tools do I need for my daily adventure?*

For example, when I go for a long day hike, I carry the following items in my daypack:

- » Water bottle and MSR Dromedary bag
- » Snacks
- » Long-sleeved merino wool shirt
- » Vest
- » Rain poncho
- » Journal and pens
- » Cell phone
- » Small Joby tripod
- » First aid kit
- » Map

When I pack my hiking bag or my photography toolkit, I feel excited and grateful for the day ahead. Being able to go on daily adventures is a privilege, and having autonomy over my daily choices and creativity is a gift.

Now it's your turn…

You might enjoy fishing, running, doodling in your journal, hiking, or cycling to work, and each of those activities requires different tools. Start by making a list of the things you'll need for your adventure.

2. UNPLUG FROM THE INTERNET AND FIND A PEACEFUL PLACE TO THINK.

"If you're serious about making an impact in the world, power down your smartphone, close your browser tabs, roll up your sleeves and get to work."
—Cal Newport

I'm sensitive to noise—both in real life and online—so it's important for me to find peaceful places to think. One of my favorite places in my hometown is Greenhorn Park in Yreka, California. I enjoy hiking in the park because it's quiet.

While I'm hiking, I don't check email, social networks, read articles, or listen to podcasts because unplugging from the Internet gives me the space to think about creative projects, my relationships, fitness goals, and more. Inevitably, good ideas surface when I'm walking in the park, so I use my journal to record my thoughts.

In *Reclaiming Conversation: The Power of Talk in the Digital Age* Sherry Turkle noted:

> Reclaiming conversation begins with reclaiming our capacity for solitude. When we reach for a phone to push reverie away, we should get into the habit of asking why. Perhaps we are not moving

toward our phones but away from something else. Are we hiding from anxiety? Are we hiding from a good idea that will demand difficult work? Are we hiding from a question that will take time to sort through?

The questions Turkle poses are valuable and thought provoking. I'd also add another question to the list: If we're always plugged into the Internet, how can we enjoy our daily adventures or find a sense of peaceful and fulfillment?

Now it's your turn…

Unplug from the Internet, and find a peaceful place to think. You could go to a local park, a church, a meditation center, a playground, or you could create a sacred space in your home.

3. NOTICE THE COLORS.

"Spring is the time of plans and projects."
—Leo Tolstoy, *Anna Karenina*

I adore capturing colors, textures, and light with my camera. For example, whether it's spring, winter, fall, or summer, I challenge myself to notice five new colors when I'm out doing chores. Then I take snapshots of the colors with my camera.

It might seem silly, but making an effort to notice new colors makes daily errands feel like an adventure. Later in the day, I'll journal about the colors that I noticed. Inevitably, writing about my observations makes me feel grateful and alive.

I can't go on epic hikes or adventures every day. However, I can make the choice to fill my day with small challenges that bring joy, gratitude, and adventure to my daily routine.

Make the time to notice new colors and to capture those colors with your camera. Then write about how the activity made you feel.

4. WORK REMOTELY.

"We work better together when we can also work alone. And we work best alone when we are undistracted."
—Sherry Turkle, *Reclaiming Conversation: The Power of Talk in a Digital Age*

In October 2015, Elizabeth Gilbert was on tour to promote her newly released book, *Big Magic: Creative Living Beyond Fear*, and around that time she shared a Facebook post about her writing process. In the post, Gilbert talked about how movement is her superpower, how she travels frequently, and that she's never written more than one book in the same house.

I'm similar to Gilbert. I like to go out into the world to gather information and inspiration for my job and creative side projects. I find inspiration and stories in nature, at coffee shops, walking around new cities, and when I talk with friends.

Over the years, I've been fortunate because I've been able to work remotely both in traditional day jobs and as a self-employed writer, photographer, and teacher. I love working from different places and spaces to see how it affects my creative process.

Try working in a different place or space and notice how it affects your creative process. Go to a:

- » Coffee shop
- » Public library
- » Conference room

- » Different corner of your office
- » Park

If your boss doesn't like the idea of remote work, try applying the concept to your personal creative projects. At my last day job, I focused on writing essays for my blog before or after work. I spent some of my non-work hours writing in various coffee shops, and when the weather was nice, I wrote in the park. It was lovely, and it gave me the opportunity to explore my community.

Experiment and have fun while you work!

5. GO FOR A WALKING MEETING.

"Walk and talk. You'll be surprised
at how fresh air drives fresh thinking."
—Nilofer Merchant

As I *write* this tiny quest, I'm hiking up a hill at a local park. I'm huffing and puffing as I climb the slope, and amazingly, the dictation feature in my phone can capture my words. When I'm walking outside, ideas flow freely. I can walk and talk into my phone, and as a bonus, I don't feel stumped for words. I use the same strategy when I have meetings on the telephone or in real life because creative ideas and solutions are generated a little more quickly.

In Nilofer Merchant's TED talk, she discussed how walking can have a big impact on your health and productivity. She said:

"Next time you have a one-on-one meeting,
make it into a "walking meeting"
— and let ideas flow while you walk and talk."

The next time you're struggling with a creative project, or have a meeting, go for a stroll. Walking alone, or with coworkers, can improve your health, generate ideas, and it can add a slice of adventure to your work day.

6. PRETEND YOU'RE A LITTLE KID, AND GO PLAY!

"Wholehearted adults play."
—Brené Brown

As a 'tween, I was more serious than the average kid. For example, I read *The Seven Habits of Highly Effective People* when I was eleven. I don't know where my serious nature came from, but that part of my personality followed me into adulthood. As a result, I forget that it's okay to play like a little kid.

When I remember to play—and schedule unstructured time into my calendar—I have more fun in my daily life. I'm also more likely to go on spontaneous adventures like having a coffee date with a friend or taking an early morning hike.

In Brené Brown's article, *Why Goofing Off Is Really Good For You*, she dared readers to:

Create a play list. Write down three activities you could do for hours on end. Mine are reading, editing photos on my computer and playing Ping-Pong with my family. Now carve out time on your calendar. Even when I'm busiest, I schedule unstructured time. It's important to protect playtime the way you protect work, church or PTA meetings.

I encourage you to follow Brené Brown's advice and create your own play list. As you brainstorm playful activities, think how these interests can add a sense of adventure into your life.

If you're stumped, try:

- » Jumping on trampoline
- » Doing a cartwheel
- » Playing Frisbee with friends
- » Laughing more often
- » Making jokes (even if they're bad)
- » Reading novels instead of non-fiction
- » Draw or doodle with your kids or the kids in your life
- » Going to a painting class
- » Reading the comics
- » Do nothing

7. TRY SOMETHING NEW.

"The big question is whether you are going to be able to say a hearty yes to your adventure."
—Joseph Campbell

Stepping outside of your comfort zone and trying something new can be scary and exciting. For example, when I created this journal I felt nervous. However, my anxiety was unfounded because I worked with an incredible designer to create the notebook, which made the creative process fun and rewarding.

With that being said, I don't ignore all my fears. Some concerns are worth listening to. For example, if my instinct tells me not to walk down a dark alley, I listen. Within reason, my fears keep me safe and away from danger.

Not all of my fears are valid, however. Producing this journal didn't endanger my life. The biggest risk was not breaking even on the production costs.

Before I try something new—especially when it comes to new creative projects and adventures—I acknowledge my fears, and then I get to work. When I name my fear and get clear on the story I'm telling myself, I'm not as scared to try something new. If I'm relaxed, instead of scared, it's easier to attempt something new.

Here are a few ideas to try:

- » Take a different route to work
- » Walk or bike to the grocery store
- » Start a 365-day project
- » Talk to a stranger
- » Start a blog
- » Develop a daily journaling practice
- » Take a 24-hour digital sabbatical
- » Start a new fitness routine

What can you add to the list?

8. PLAN A WEEKEND GETAWAY.

"Evolution intended us to be travelers … Settlement for any length of time, in cave or castle, has at best been … a drop in the ocean of evolutionary time."
—Bruce Chatwin, *Anatomy of Restlessness*

During the summer, Logan and I have time to go on more adventures. We'll go on epic hikes, day trips, and we plan weekend getaways. For example, during the summer of 2015, Logan and I celebrated our 12th year of marriage, and we decided to drive to Jacksonville, OR for an adventure. The trip wasn't planned, and we weren't sure if we would stay the night or come home in the evening. Jacksonville is only a one-hour drive from our home so a day trip would have been feasible, but we packed an overnight bag just in case we stayed.

When we arrived in Jacksonville, we stopped at Pony Espresso for coffee, looked at a local map, and checked hotel prices on our phones. Priceline had a few inexpensive rooms listed, and we chose to stay at a tiny cottage.

While we were in Jacksonville, we had fantastic food, beer, coffee, and ice cream. It was a treat to eat at restaurants, but the best part of the trip was spending time with Logan. We walked all over the city, through the park, and had long talks about the trajectory of our lives. Our overnight adventure was special and unique.

Now it's your turn...

Research a place you want to visit and plan a weekend getaway.

As you plan your getaway:

» Be flexible about the destination

» Think about taking a trip close to home

» Consider camping (it can be inexpensive and fun)

» Try to take a 3-day weekend

» Keep it simple, and don't get too bogged down with logistics and planning

9. NOTICE THE BEAUTY IN YOUR HOME.

" ... what our home looks like may change drastically through the years. But always, what remains constant is our deep need for home, and the importance of it in our lives. Play and work, connection and family, retreat and sanctuary—home is where this happens."

—Amanda Blake Soule, *Taproot Magazine ISSUE 16 | SHELTER*

Whether I'm living in my tiny house on wheels or in a small apartment, I take time to notice the beauty in my home. Sometimes, I'll make a game of it and challenge myself to notice three or more lovely details about my home, like:

- » The art and photographs on my walls
- » How the morning light hits my standing desk
- » The purr of the heater on cold mornings
- » The handmade quilt on my bed
- » The beauty of an unmade bed with a cat cuddled in the sheets
- » My clutter-free countertops

I feel joyful, thankful, and a little more adventurous when I appreciate the belongings in my home and roof over my head.

What are three things that make your home beautiful?

If you're having trouble with this exercise, think about how you can add small slices of beauty to your living space.

You could:

>> Rearrange your furniture

>> De-clutter your office, countertops, or closet

>> Color-code your bookshelf

>> Create a shelf dedicated to your favorite plants

10. VISIT A UNIQUE PLACE IN YOUR COMMUNITY.

" … adventure starts the moment I leave my door."
—Gloria Steinem, *My Life on the Road*

In October 2015, I spent the day wandering around Dunsmuir, CA—a small town near our home in Yreka. I ate good food, went to Hedge Creek Falls, and unexpectedly stopped at the Dunsmuir City Park.

The detour was worth my time because the Dunsmuir City Park has a charming botanical garden and a walking trail that runs along the Sacramento River. It was a stunning fall day, and I felt like I'd walked into a postcard. The golden aspen leaves were falling off the trees and people were scattered along the river fishing.

In the afternoon, I attended the Dunsmuir Art Walk. Most of the storefronts—even the stores that are usually closed and empty—were open and filled with art. Seeing so many people exploring the little town of Dunsmuir made me happy. The day was inexpensive, magical, and memorable.

Are there unique places or spaces in your community that you haven't visited? Make a list of those places and visit one or two sites this month. If you're able to visit more places, that's great! If not, save your list for future adventures.

If you aren't sure what sites to visit, here are a few ideas:

- » Attend an art walk
- » Go to a local museum
- » Try a new restaurant or café
- » Ask locals for hiking tips

Finally, pay attention to your surroundings. If you see something interesting, like a park or a cool café, take a detour and explore.

11. START A DAILY PHOTOGRAPHY PROJECT.

"You can choose to see every day as an opportunity for adventure, and welcome little moments of whimsy, or you can drudge through every day like it's a chore, totally numb."
—Amanda Sandlin

After my step-dad, Mahlon, died in June 2012, I decided to focus on a creative project to honor Mahlon's memory. I began a daily photography project called My Morning View on January 1, 2013. Since then, I've been taking a daily photo of my morning view with my coffee cup in the frame.

I decided on this photographic topic because Mahlon and I loved coffee and being outside. Also, choosing a theme to photograph gave my series structure. In addition, the theme enabled me to consistently photograph my view, whether I was at home or traveling.

In addition, I decided to use my iPhone to take daily snapshots. I love iPhone photography, and I wanted a camera that would always be with me. I wanted my photography project to be a source of joy, so taking and sharing my photos had to be easy. Otherwise, the project wouldn't have been part of my daily creative routine.

And, last but not least, my photography series continues to give meaning to the grief I experienced, and it's fostered creative self-discipline, optimism, joy, and a sense of adventure in my everyday life.

Brainstorm ways a daily photography project can infuse a sense of purpose and adventure into your daily life.

Once you start taking photos, remember to:

- » Choose your camera.
- » Pick a subject to photograph.
- » Seek out creative inspiration.
- » Decide on the length of your project.
- » Incorporate your photography practice into your daily routine.
- » Use your photography project to facilitate everyday adventures. Taking daily photos is a fantastic reason to visit new places in your community.

12. ENJOY THE MOMENT.

"The purpose of life is to live it, to taste experience to the utmost, to reach out eagerly and without fear for newer and richer experience."
—Eleanor Roosevelt

In late 2015, I drove my grandma-in-law, Pat, to a doctor's appointment in Medford, Oregon. The drive from her home outside of Yreka, CA to Medford takes about one-hour. On the drive back home, we talked about a variety of topics including the healthcare system, my step-dad's death in 2012, and what it means to live well into old age.

I asked Pat, "If you could give advice to an 18-year-old, advice that would help that person live a good life, what would you say?"

Pat offered the following:

1. Spend time with your loved ones.

2. Enjoy each moment because you never know what's going to happen next.

3. Do the things you want to before your body or mind gives out.

No matter what your age, Pat's advice is invaluable, and her words of wisdom are at the heart of this journal.

Each day can be an adventure, especially when you spend time with loved ones, savor each moment, and do what you enjoy. Whether you're going on an epic trip or seeking out the familiar, an adventure state of mind is all about staying open to whatever comes along. It all starts the moment you walk out your front door.

RESOURCES

Throughout this book, I mentioned articles, books, websites, inspiring people, and more. You'll find links to those resources here: www.rowdykittens.com/everydayadventures

ABOUT TAMMY STROBEL

Tammy Strobel is a writer, photographer, teacher, and the founder of RowdyKittens.com. She created her blog, RowdyKittens.com, in late 2007 to improve her writing and to share her story. Tammy spends her free time taking photos, swimming, walking, and hanging out with friends and family.

Tammy lives in northern California with her husband, Logan, and two cats. You can follow her adventures at rowdykittens.com.